LIVING WITH THE DINOSAURS

SPIDERS

LIVED WITH THE DINOSAURS!

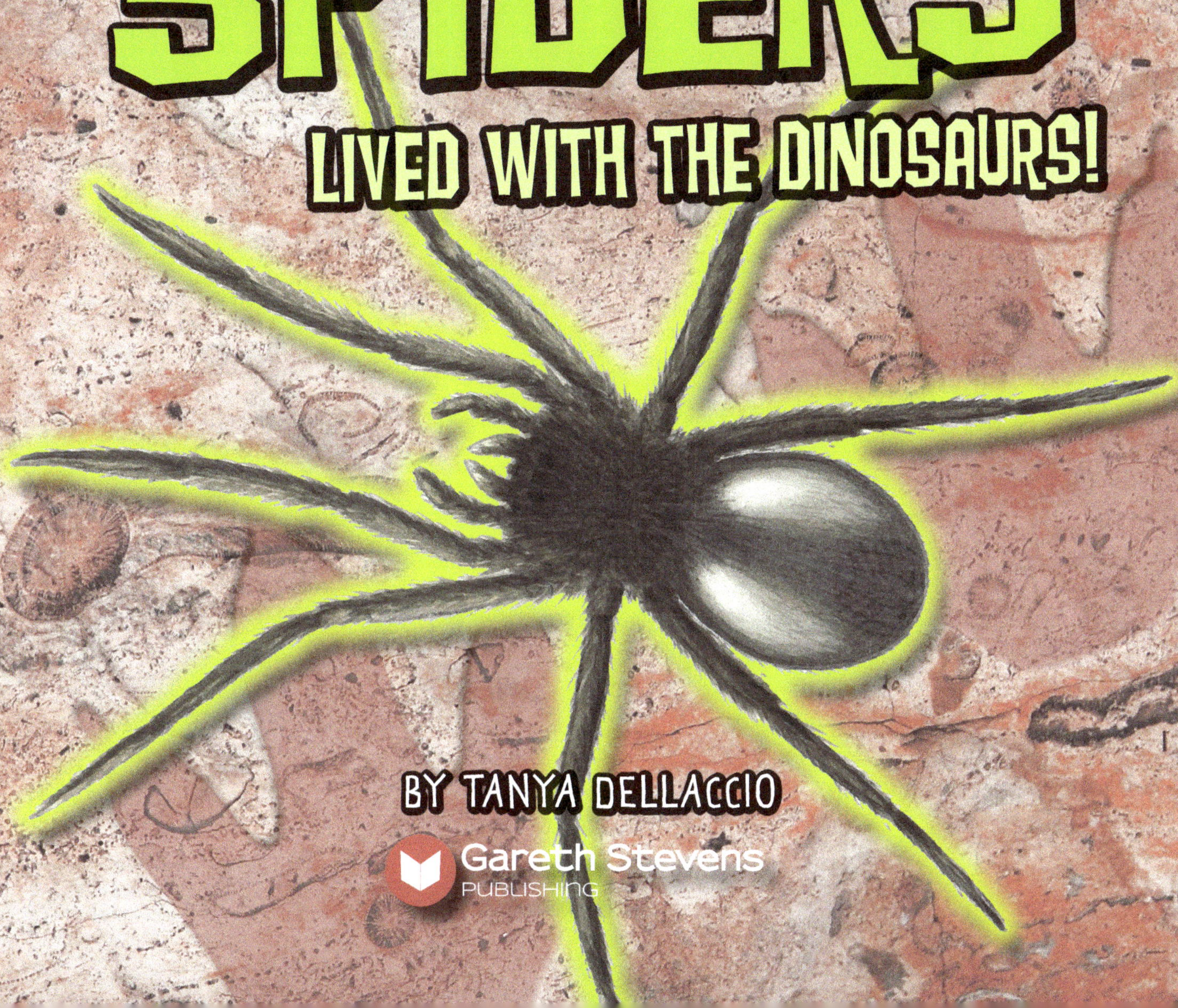

BY TANYA DELLACCIO

Gareth Stevens
PUBLISHING

Please visit our website, www.garethstevens.com. For a free color catalog of all our high-quality books, call toll free 1-800-542-2595 or fax 1-877-542-2596.

Cataloging-in-Publication Data

Names: Dellaccio, Tanya.
Title: Spiders lived with the dinosaurs! / Tanya Dellaccio.
Description: New York : Gareth Stevens Publishing, 2017. | Series: Living with the dinosaurs | Includes index.
Identifiers: ISBN 9781482456813 (pbk.) | ISBN 9781482456844 (library bound) | ISBN 9781482456820 (6 pack)
Subjects: LCSH: Spiders–Juvenile literature.
Classification: LCC QL458.4 D45 2017 | DDC 595.4'4–dc23

First Edition

Published in 2017 by
Gareth Stevens Publishing
111 East 14th Street, Suite 349
New York, NY 10003

Designer: Laura Bowen
Editor: Therese Shea

Photo credits: Cover, p. 1 (spider) Alan Baker/Getty Images; cover, p. 1 (footprints) nemlaza/Shutterstock.com; cover, pp. 1–24 (background) Natalia Davidovich/Shutterstock.com; cover, pp. 1–24 (stone boxes) Daria Yakovleva/Shutterstock.com; pp. 4, 21 (main) Herschel Hoffmeyer/Shutterstock.com; p. 5 File Upload Bot/Wikimedia Commons; p. 7 (main) PaulASelden/Wikimedia Commons; p. 7 (inset) fivespots/Shutterstock.com; p. 9 Auscape/UIG/Getty Images; p. 10 Nancy Tripp Photography/Shutterstock.com; p. 11 Gerry van der Walt/Shutterstock.com; p. 12 Hectonichus/Shutterstock.com; p. 13 Henrik Larsson/Shutterstock.com; p. 15 (main) Tomatito/Shutterstock.com; p. 15 (inset) Stocktrek Images/Getty Images; p. 16 Nobumichi Tamura/Stocktrek Images/Getty Images; p. 17 Katarina Christenson/Shutterstock.com; p. 18 NataBene/Shutterstock.com; p. 19 (top left and right) Cathy Keifer/Shutterstock.com; p. 19 (bottom) Sarah2/Shutterstock.com; p. 20 papkin/Shutterstock.com; p. 21 (amber) Layne Kennedy/Getty Images.

Printed in the United States of America

CPSIA compliance information: Batch #CW17GS: For further information contact Gareth Stevens, New York, New York at 1-800-542-2595.

CONTENTS

Words in the glossary appear in **bold** type the first time they are used in the text.

ANCIENT SPIDERS

Spiders have lived on Earth for a very long time. They've been around for at least 380 million years! Did you know they existed at the same time the dinosaurs did? Even though dinosaurs are now **extinct**, spiders have found ways to survive.

Spider **fossils** date back to **prehistoric** times. They give us a picture of what spiders were like among the dinosaurs—and before the dinosaurs. They're proof that spiders have always been incredible creatures!

THE PREHISTORIC WORLD

Spiderlike bugs date back to about 400 million years ago, but scientists don't think "true spiders" appeared until 380 million years ago.

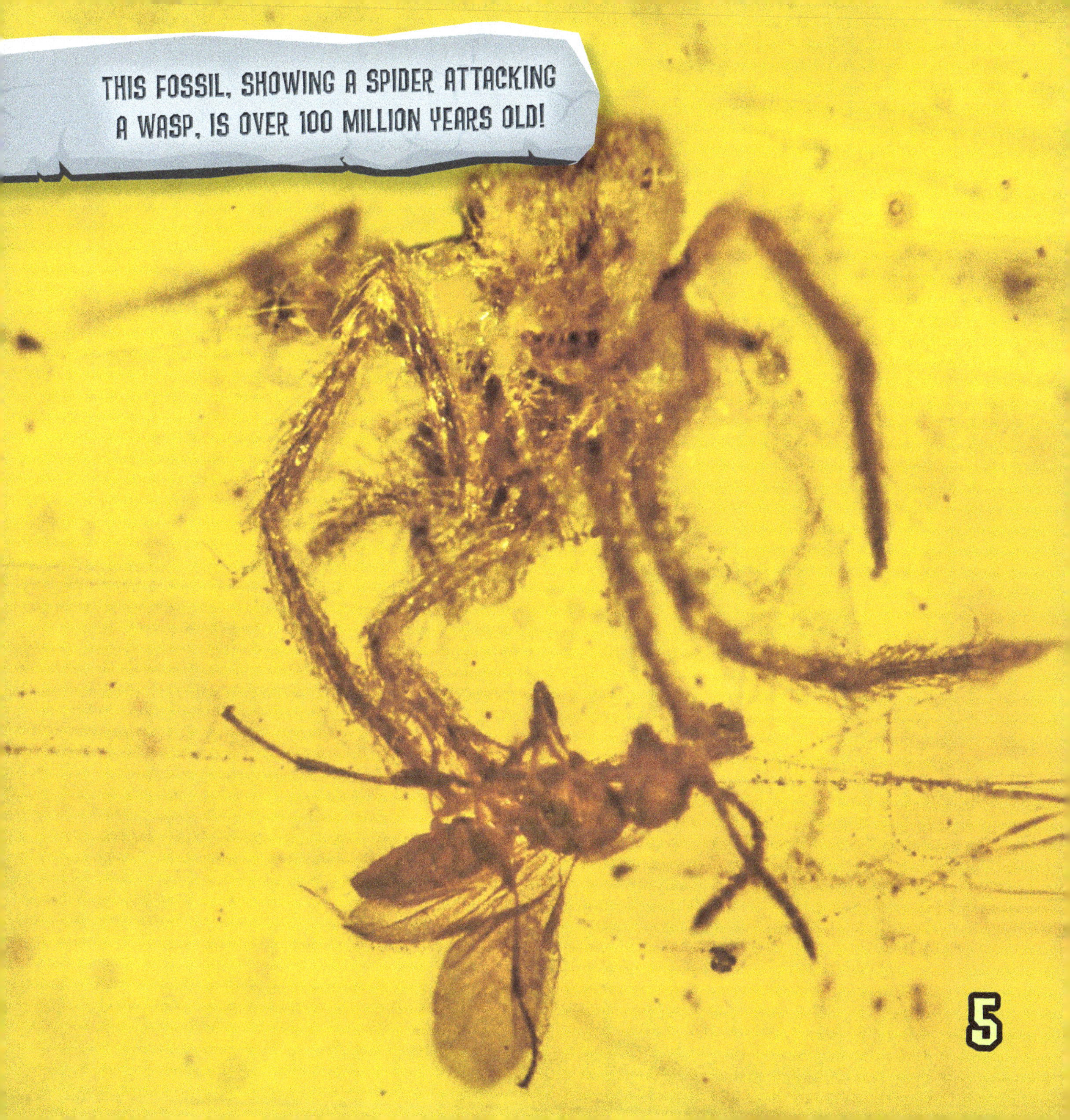

THIS FOSSIL, SHOWING A SPIDER ATTACKING A WASP, IS OVER 100 MILLION YEARS OLD!

SO MANY LEGS!

Spiders are part of the arachnid family. Many other eight-legged bugs belong in this group, including ticks, scorpions, and mites. Most arachnids are small. The spider *Patu digua* is just 15/1000 inch (0.38 mm) long, while the Goliath bird-eating spider has a leg span of up to 12 inches (30 cm)!

The largest spider fossil that's been found is the prehistoric spider named *Mongolarachne jurassica* (mon-goh-luh-RAK-nee juh-RAA-sih-kuh). *M. jurassica*'s body was 1 inch (2.5 cm) wide and its legs were 2.5 inches (6.4 cm) long.

THE PREHISTORIC WORLD

Scientists think *M. jurassica* only hunted at night. This would have made it harder for predators—which probably included some dinosaurs—to see and catch it.

THIS FOSSIL BELOW SHOWS BOTH A MALE (LEFT) AND A FEMALE (RIGHT) *M. JURASSICA*. IT'S THE LARGEST SPIDER FOSSIL FOUND YET, BUT SMALL COMPARED TO THE MODERN GOLIATH BIRD-EATING SPIDER.

SUPERSILK

Scientists have counted around 40,000 different species, or types, of spiders today. An **adaptation** that they all share is the ability to produce threads of silk, thanks to body parts called spinnerets.

The silk is made of a kind of **protein**, which makes it very tough. It's also elastic, which means it has the ability to stretch without breaking. It can stretch to become about 30 percent longer than its original length. Spiders produce different kinds of silk for different purposes. Spiders wouldn't have survived without their silk!

THE PREHISTORIC WORLD

The Tasmanian cave spider is a species of spider alive today. It's thought to be directly related to prehistoric spiders!

SPIDER SILK IS THE STRONGEST MATERIAL MADE BY A LIVING THING. THERE ARE AT LEAST SEVEN KINDS OF SPIDER SILK, THOUGH MOST SPIDERS CAN ONLY MAKE THREE OR FOUR.

Tasmanian cave spider

THE WEBS THEY WEAVE

The most famous use of a spider's silk is its web, though only half of spider species make them. The oldest fossilized spider web is at least 130 million years old! A spider's sticky web traps prey flying or walking by. The spider then uses silk to wrap prey until the spider is ready to eat.

Spiders mostly eat **insects**. However, some larger species can eat small animals, such as frogs, lizards, or even birds! Spiders can also catch predators such as birds and wasps in their superstrong webs.

spider wrapping its prey

THIS BIRD GOT CAUGHT IN A SPIDER WEB. THE WEB-SPINNING ADAPTATION HAS HELPED SPIDERS SURVIVE AMONG LARGER, STRONGER ANIMALS.

AMBUSH SPIDERS

Not all spiders use webs to catch prey. Hunting spiders have good eyesight to find and capture prey. They use it, too. Jumping spiders are a kind of hunting spider that can leap 30 times the length of their own body onto their prey! Crab spiders are hunting spiders that use **camouflage**. They hide on flowers the same color as their body and wait for prey.

Scientists think the 300-million-year-old prehistoric spider called *Cryptomartus hindi*, or *C. hindi*, was like the crab spider. Both used their front legs to catch—and crush!—prey.

C. hindi fossil

THE PREHISTORIC WORLD

A spider called *E. prestivicii* lived before the dinosaurs, about 300 million years ago. It had spikes on its back, probably to scare amphibian predators!

C. HINDI MIGHT HAVE LOOKED MUCH LIKE THIS CRAB SPIDER.

SPIDER VISION

A spider often has eight eyes, though some have six or fewer. While hunting spiders have good eyesight, most web-spinning spiders don't. They use other senses to make up for that, such as touch and taste.

Spiders often use **vibrations** on their web and on the ground to tell them about the world. In fact, scientists have discovered that spiders pluck their web, then wait to feel the vibrations that come back. The vibrations tell them if the web needs to be fixed and about prey stuck in it.

THE PREHISTORIC WORLD

Like many spiders, dinosaurs didn't have good eyesight. The *Carcharodontosaurus* (kar-kar-uh-don-tuh-SAWR-uhs) couldn't see well at all. It's thought that this meat eater hunted using its sense of smell!

MOST SPIDERS HAVE POOR EYESIGHT. HOWEVER, THEY HAVE SPECIAL LEGS THAT CAN SENSE VIBRATIONS—AND EVEN SMELLS IN THE AIR!

Carcharodontosaurus

AND POISON, TOO

All spiders have jaws called chelicerae (kuh-LIH-suh-ree). These jaws end in **fangs**! The fangs work like needles. Most spiders produce a liquid poison called venom. When the spider's fangs stick into its prey, venom flows into the creature.

The venom often **paralyzes** prey, so it won't fight back. Spider venom may turn a bug's insides into mush, too. Spiders don't eat what they catch—they actually drink their prey! Few spiders have venom strong enough to harm people, though.

Sinornithosaurus

THE PREHISTORIC WORLD

For a time, some scientists thought the dinosaur called *Sinornithosaurus* (syn-ohr-nihth-uh-SAWR-uhs) was venomous. However, there's no proof of this or any dinosaur producing venom.

SPIDER VENOM IS ANOTHER ADAPTATION THAT HAS LONG HELPED SPIDERS FIGHT PREY AND PREDATORS LARGER THAN THEMSELVES.

BALLOONING

Spiders can live just about anywhere. They're found on every **continent** except Antarctica and on mountains as high as 16,000 feet (4,880 m)! Some species even live on—or in—water.

Ballooning is a **behavior** that takes spiders to new locations. It's one way they keep spreading around the world. The spider, often a baby called a spiderling, throws a thread of silk into the air and allows itself to be carried by the wind.

THE ADAPTATION OF BALLOONING MEANT SPIDERS COULD ESCAPE HARMFUL CONDITIONS IN THEIR SURROUNDINGS. PERHAPS THAT'S WHY DINOSAURS ARE EXTINCT AND SPIDERS AREN'T!

Spider Silk's Many Uses

catch prey in web

wrap prey to keep it from getting away

wrap eggs to keep them safe

ballooning to travel to a new place

make nest

trap predators in web

make trap for prey on ground

HOW DID THEY SURVIVE?

Some spider species lay more than 1,000 eggs at a time. This means more of these spiders have a chance of surviving than bug species that lay fewer eggs. Spiders have another cool adaptation. They can lose a leg and easily regrow it as they grow and **molt**.

Spiders may be small, but they have amazing adaptations to keep them alive! They prove that you don't have to be large to survive. Would *T. rex* be alive today if it had had spiderlike adaptations?

HOPEFULLY, MORE SPIDER FOSSILS WILL BE FOUND IN THE FUTURE TO HELP US BETTER UNDERSTAND HOW THESE INCREDIBLE ARACHNIDS CHANGED OVER TIME.

GLOSSARY

adaptation: a change in an animal that makes it better able to live in its surroundings

behavior: the way an animal acts

camouflage: colors, shapes, or behaviors that allow an animal to hide in its surroundings

continent: one of Earth's seven great landmasses

extinct: no longer living

fang: a long, pointed tooth

fossil: the hardened marks or remains of plants and animals that formed over thousands or millions of years

insect: a small, often winged, animal with six legs and a three-part body

molt: to lose a covering of hair, feathers, or skin and replace it with new growth in the same place

paralyze: to make something lose the ability to move

prehistoric: before recorded history

protein: a necessary element found in all living things

vibration: a rapid movement back and forth

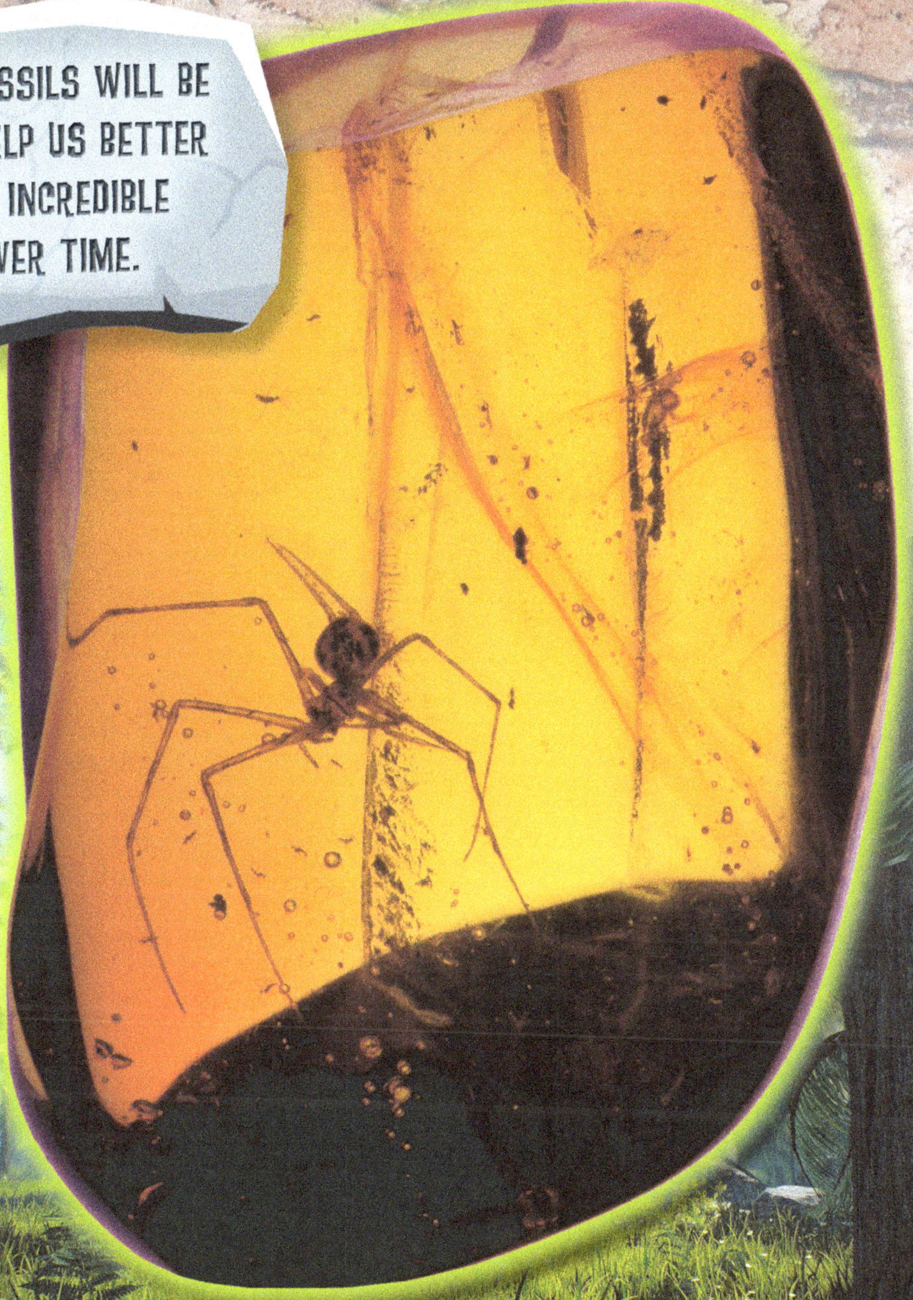

FOR MORE INFORMATION

BOOKS

Bishop, Celeste. *Scrambling Spiders.* New York, NY: PowerKids Press, 2015.

Bodden, Valerie. *Spider.* Mankato, MN: Creative Education, 2015.

WEBSITES

Prehistoric Spiders
www.enkivillage.com/prehistoric-spiders.html
This site explores some of the prehistoric spiders in this book.

Spider Sense: Fast Facts on Extreme Arachnids
news.nationalgeographic.com/news/2004/06/0623_040623_spiderfacts.html
Find out more fun facts about spiders here.

Types of Spiders & Spider Facts
www.livescience.com/22122-types-of-spiders.html
Read about different types of spiders.

Publisher's note to educators and parents: Our editors have carefully reviewed these websites to ensure that they are suitable for students. Many websites change frequently, however, and we cannot guarantee that a site's future contents will continue to meet our high standards of quality and educational value. Be advised that students should be closely supervised whenever they access the Internet.

INDEX